MW01178600

Dust

by Billy Goda

A SAMUEL FRENCH ACTING EDITION

SAMUEL
FRENCH
FOUNDED 1830

NEW YORK HOLLYWOOD LONDON TORONTO

SAMUELFRENCH.COM

IMPORTANT BILLING AND CREDIT REQUIREMENTS

All producers of *DUST* *must* give credit to the Author of the Play in all programs distributed in connection with performances of the Play, and in all instances in which the title of the Play appears for the purposes of advertising, publicizing or otherwise exploiting the Play and/or a production. The name of the Author *must* appear on a separate line on which no other name appears, immediately following the title and *must* appear in size of type not less than fifty percent of the size of the title type.

In addition the following credit *must* be given in all programs and publicity information distributed in association with this piece:

Originally produced Off Broadway by
Roger Alan Gindi and Cassidy Productions

WESTSIDE THEATRE
(DOWNSTAIRS)

ROGER ALAN GINDI and CASSIDY PRODUCTIONS

present

RICHARD   HUNTER
MASUR   FOSTER

in

DUST

a new thriller by
BILLY GODA

with

LAURA E.	CURTIS	JOHN
CAMPBELL	McCLARIN	SCHIAPPA

Set Design	Costume Design	Lighting Design	Sound Design
CALEB	THERESA	CHARLES	SHARATH
WERTENBAKER	SQUIRE	FOSTER	PATEL

Fight Direction	Production Manager	Production Stage Manager
RICK	ADURO	PAMELA
SORDELET	PRODUCTIONS	EDINGTON

Press Representatives	Marketing
KEITH SHERMAN	HHC
ASSOCIATES	MARKETING

General Manager	Casting
GINDI THEATRICAL	JANET
MANAGEMENT	FOSTER

Directed By
SCOTT ZIGLER

CAST

(in order of appearance)

Martin Stone . . . . RICHARD MASUR
Zeke Catchman . . . . HUNTER FOSTER
Bobby Lawton . . . . CURTIS McCLARIN
Jenny Stone . . . . LAURA E. CAMPBELL
Ralph . . . . JOHN SCHIAPPA
Digs . . . . CURTIS McCLARIN
Tyler . . . . JOHN SCHIAPPA

UNDERSTUDIES
Understudies never substitute for listed players
unless a specific announcement is made at the time of the appearance.

For Zeke and Ralph/Tyler—THOMAS MATTHEW KELLEY; for Martin and
Ralph/Tyler—KEVIN C. LOOMIS; for Bobby/Digs and Ralph/Tyler—DeLANCE
MINEFEE; for Jenny—ELIZABETH OLSEN

CHARACTERS

ZEKE CATCHMAN – A volatile, yet likable, thirty year-old man. He is well-built and can handle himself in a confrontation.

MARTIN STONE – An overweight man in his early sixties. He is a very wealthy man who is used to getting what he wants. He is troubled by his declining health.

JENNY STONE (Martin's daughter) – A thin, attractive nineteen year-old girl. She has the unusual combination of kindness and biting sarcasm.

BOBBY LAWTON – A thirty year-old black man who is a parole officer. He is a sincere, honest man.

RALPH – A confident, large man in his late thirties. He is Martin's body guard.

DIGS – A black man in his late twenties. He is a drug dealer who finds humor in most situations.

TYLER – A large man who is out to intimidate.

Five actors are needed for this play:
Bobby and Digs can be played by the same actor.
Ralph and Tyler can be played by the same actor.

SETTING

A stylized set should be used to keep the playing area as fluid as possible. Each change of scene should be suggested by the shifting of key furniture pieces and props.

ACT I

Scene I

(The fitness center at the Essex House, an expensive hotel. It is six a.m. and **MARTIN STONE,** *a man in his early sixties, is walking on a treadmill. He is the only patron there.* **ZEKE CATCHMAN,** *a thirty year-old handy man, is seated at the desk reading the newspaper.)*

MARTIN. Could you come here please.

*(***ZEKE** *puts down his paper and walks over.)*

ZEKE. What can I do for you, Mr. Stone?

MARTIN. *(pointing up)* What's that?

ZEKE. What?

MARTIN. Up there.

ZEKE. That?

MARTIN. Yes.

ZEKE. An air vent.

MARTIN. What's in the air vent?

ZEKE. Is this a trick question? 'Cause I'm gonna have to say air.

*(***MARTIN** *stares at* **ZEKE,** *making him uncomfortable.)*

MARTIN. That's dust.

ZEKE. You misled me.

MARTIN. How so?

ZEKE. You said in the vent, but you meant what's on the vent. If you had said on, I might have said dust.

MARTIN. Is this a joke?

ZEKE. You tell me.

MARTIN. You pay what I'm paying to live here and you don't expect to have dust caked on a vent.

ZEKE. It's not caked...

MARTIN. It's dust.

ZEKE. *(after a moment)* I'll call house-keeping and have someone come clean it.

(ZEKE starts to walk away.)

MARTIN. Don't you think it's wrong?

ZEKE. *(laughing)* Wrong? No, not at all. It happens.

MARTIN. Doesn't it mean people aren't paying attention to detail? That this hotel isn't meeting it's standards?

(no response)

You lost a star this past year, services all around this place are slacking, but I keep putting up my people when they come to town...

ZEKE. *(joking)* Isn't that swell of you.

MARTIN. What did you just say...

ZEKE. Is there a camera here? Someone gonna jump out and tell me I'm on a new reality show...

MARTIN. There's no damn camera.

(MARTIN shuts off the treadmill. He stares ZEKE down.)

What's your name again?

(reading the name tag)

Zeke...

ZEKE. Catchman...

MARTIN. Zeke Catchman.

ZEKE. I'll call house-keeping...

MARTIN. And that solves this problem, Zeke Catchman?

ZEKE. I get your point...

MARTIN. I don't think you do...

ZEKE. Relax, Mr. Stone, it's all good...

MARTIN. Relax? Did you just tell me to relax...

ZEKE. If a little dust has you all freaked out, it's a sure sign that a few deep breaths are needed.

MARTIN. So I'm just a crazy old man, a fool causing problems...

ZEKE. That's not what...

MARTIN. That's what I'm hearing!

ZEKE. I'm only saying, if this is the worse that happens to you today, you're not having such a bad time of it.

(pause)

MARTIN. You're not a natural fit in the customer service industry, Zeke Catchman.

ZEKE. I'm speaking my mind too much, not kissing up enough?

MARTIN. I'm not looking for kissing up.

ZEKE. What is it you're looking for?

(no response)

You should be looking to work out a little harder, instead of giving the white glove treatment.

MARTIN. No, this position here doesn't seem to suit you.

ZEKE. I'm only filling in here, a little over time. It's a good thing I'm employed as a handyman, right?

(ZEKE laughs.)

MARTIN. *(after a moment)* Be handy enough to clean those vents.

ZEKE. I'll get house-keeping right on it, get them to wipe them all down. They'll make 'em sparkling.

MARTIN. I want you to clean them.

ZEKE. Come again?

MARTIN. You make them "sparkling."

(pause)

Get your bottle of Windex, a rag, and a step ladder...

ZEKE. You want me to get a hula-hoop also?

MARTIN. What are you...

ZEKE. So I can jump through that for you?

MARTIN. You can do the hoop jumping after the vents shine.

(Pause. No one moves.)

The camera's running, son, what are you going to do?

ZEKE. I'll call.

MARTIN. I want you to do it.

I want you to learn some respect.

(After a moment, **ZEKE** *walks over to his desk, picks up the phone and calls.)*

ZEKE. How you doing, this is Zeke in the fitness center…

*(***MARTIN*** hangs up the phone.)*

MARTIN. What part of you cleaning them didn't you understand?

ZEKE. I understand you just fine. Your method of teaching me respect is where the problem lies.

(pause)

MARTIN. How long have you been working here?

ZEKE. Over six months.

MARTIN. You like this job?

ZEKE. I do.

MARTIN. Be easy for me to have you fired.

ZEKE. What happened to you, Mr. Stone?

When your cable went out, and I came up and fixed it, we talked. Do you remember?

MARTIN. I remember I gave you a generous tip.

ZEKE. And I thanked you.

You told me how you came from a tough part of Philly, grew up with very little, and that with some sweat a person can get ahead. That you started on the bottom rung at an investment firm…

MARTIN. And now I run my own hedge fund. Yes…

ZEKE. Your story was kind of inspirational – a regular guy making it big…

MARTIN. I busted my ass for years…

ZEKE. How do you go from being like this to threatening my life situation…

MARTIN. And I'm not going to stand for some young punk trying to make me feel like an idiot, showing me no damn respect!

ZEKE. You started barking before I disrespected you, if I even did.

(*pause*)

Listen, I'm sorry if I was rude. I was only fooling with you, because I felt comfortable around you. It's early, six a.m., we're both tired, things get misunderstood…

MARTIN. You're going to clean those vents, Zeke.

(*pause*)

(**ZEKE** *looks down and starts reading the newspaper. He turns a page, as* **MARTIN** *slams his hand down on top of it.* **ZEKE** *looks at him.*)

ZEKE. You're a tough man, Mr. Stone.

MARTIN. You have no idea.

ZEKE. The way you slammed your hand down just now, you gotta cut that out, you're scaring me. I just might shed a tear.

MARTIN. You're a real wise-ass.

ZEKE. You inspire me.

I'd appreciate removing your hand, so I can look through the want ads.

MARTIN. You're willing to lose your job?

ZEKE. I have no choice.

I own a mirror. I still have to look in it.

MARTIN. Clean those fucking vents.

ZEKE. (*standing – threatening*) Get your damn hand off my paper.

MARTIN. You should take a few deep breaths, relax, you seem awfully uptight.

(*After a moment,* **MARTIN** *removes his hand.*)

Your job's history.

ZEKE. If I lose this job, it doesn't end there.

MARTIN. Are you threatening me?

ZEKE. I'm no deer in the headlights.

MARTIN. And if I get you fired?

ZEKE. It doesn't end there.

(lights down)

(end scene)

Scene II

(It is the early evening at ZEKE*'s small studio apartment. The main piece of furniture is a futon, which is now folded into a couch.* ZEKE *is there with* BOBBY, *a thirty year-old black man.* BOBBY *is a long time friend of* ZEKE*'s as well as being his parole officer.* BOBBY *will walk around, subtly looking the place over.)*

BOBBY. …Why didn't you just clean the damn vents?

ZEKE. Would you?

(no response)

He'll get his.

BOBBY. What? What are you telling me…

ZEKE. Not from me, Bobby. You don't have to worry about that.

BOBBY. You're not gonna do anything stupid?

ZEKE. I just mean he'll get his in a karma sort of way.

BOBBY. If you screw up, as your probation officer, I'm gonna have to come down on you.

ZEKE. You've made that clear.

BOBBY. You'll end up back inside.

ZEKE. I ain't going back in there, not ever.

(pause)

BOBBY. You still clean?

ZEKE. As a whistle. I wonder where that expression came from. Whistles are not clean – people blowing in them, getting their spit all over…

BOBBY. But you're tempted?

ZEKE. *(after a moment)* Yeah, of course, I'm tempted. Probably always will be.

BOBBY. I appreciate your honesty.

*(*BOBBY, *who has been looking the place over, pulls out a small rubber hose from the garbage pail. It looks like it could be used to tie an arm off for heroin.)*

What's this, Zeke?

ZEKE. That why you wanted to meet here at the last minute? See if I might leave something lying around…

BOBBY. Tell me what it is.

ZEKE. A hose from a fish tank. It has a leak in it.

*(**BOBBY** looks doubtful.)*

Go ahead, keep searching – open some drawers, the closet, behind the toilet is always a good spot. Anywhere you want.

(no response)

I just want some fish swimming around, colorful ones. Just want to build a nice little kingdom – it's peaceful. Tanks under the sink, and now I can't afford to fill it.

(pause)

BOBBY. Have you gone to any of your old haunts?

ZEKE. No, no reason to.

BOBBY. A lot of times, when things go wrong, that's where someone feels most comfortable, most at home – making their lives a shamble…

ZEKE. It's not gonna happen.

BOBBY. I'd feel a lot better if you were in a twelve step…

ZEKE. We've been over that.

BOBBY. If you do, if you feel that urge, you call me.

*(Pause, as **BOBBY** stares at **ZEKE**, making him uncomfortable.)*

ZEKE. You want a beer or something?

BOBBY. *(after a moment)* I'm all right.

ZEKE. How's Kathy doing?

BOBBY. She's fine.

ZEKE. And Bobby Jr.?

BOBBY. He's beautiful, running around like a madman. I just got him a mitt.

ZEKE. Hope it's not a catcher's mitt.

(joking) Hope you're not trying to make him a fat fuck behind the plate like his old man.

BOBBY. *(laughing)* It's not a catcher's mitt.

ZEKE. *(after a moment)* We had a good team.

BOBBY. Yeah, we did.

ZEKE. Rachel was at all our games.

I took my bike out the other day, drove to Ardsley, to her house.

I didn't knock. I just sat there.

(after a moment)

When I was inside, I kept thinking about her.

BOBBY. You guys were pretty tight.

ZEKE. Kept thinking if I hadn't scared her off…

BOBBY. *(after a moment)* You're starting out again, starting fresh. You can make amends.

That's one of the twelve steps.

ZEKE. Sounds like a good one.

BOBBY. It's good for you to remember what you once had, once were, then you can picture being that person again.

But don't be dreaming about starting things with her. That's dangerous. That only leads to disappointment. You have to realize she's probably moved on with her life.

ZEKE. Why are you trying to help? Yeah, I know we were friends in high school, but we weren't that close.

BOBBY. You're my nigger.

ZEKE. *(laughing)* What? I'm your nigger?

BOBBY. That's right.

That night I was hanging out with some friends in front of the Pizzeria, and those guys from Dobbs drove over looking for a fight…

ZEKE. Fighting wasn't your forte…

BOBBY. There were four of them, four big fucks. They started talking trash; they started pushing people. Then they got to me. They said, "Lookie here, we got a nigger…" It was nigger this and nigger that. I looked around and my friends had all backed off…

ZEKE. That's what you get from hanging out with the drama club.

BOBBY. I looked around and saw you sitting on the curb with Grant, eating an ice-cream cone. I thought I was gonna get an ass-kicking, cause I wouldn't back away. Then you came over and said...

ZEKE. "Look at me, I'm a nigger too."

BOBBY. You said, "Us niggers, we stick together, so if you ugly fucks want to throw down..."

ZEKE. "You might as well start with this nigger in front of you."

BOBBY. They talked some shit, but...

ZEKE. But they got in their car and drove away.

BOBBY. That's right.

(ZEKE and BOBBY bump fists.)

ZEKE. *(after a moment – laughing)* So you requested my case, cause you think you owe me one, all the way back from high school?

You don't owe me anything. I was stoned, hanging out, fighting's something I'm good at...

BOBBY. That's all it was, a good time brawl?

(No response.)

You just wanted to have a little fun?

ZEKE. I couldn't stand it.

You still don't owe me.

BOBBY. I know that. I know I don't. But it let me know you're a good man. Something you've proved to me many times.

ZEKE. Same thing you're trying to prove to me with that story. You're a clever rabbit, aren't you, Bobby?

BOBBY. Things can get lost – people get older, forget about what's inside of them.

You've messed up, Zeke, but you're a good man who's messed up. When I see a good man, I do what I can to help. That's why I requested your case.

ZEKE. *(after a moment)* I ain't so good anymore.

BOBBY. We'll find out.

ZEKE. When that guy at the gym was pushing my buttons…

BOBBY. But you did the right thing.

ZEKE. Yeah, I guess I did.

BOBBY. And now you're going to let it go.

(no response)

Are you planning something?

ZEKE. No, no plans.

BOBBY. That's good.

Now you have to be careful, you're going to have a lot of free time while you're job hunting. Free time can be a dangerous thing.

ZEKE. I'm not gonna slip. You don't have to worry.

(pause)

BOBBY. I have this friend, Linda Tynes, I want you to call her. She might be able to help with some work.

*(**BOBBY** hands **ZEKE** a business card.)*

ZEKE. Thanks, Bobby.

What are you gonna write in your report?

BOBBY. That I met with Zeke Catchman, and he's staying clean, trying to do the right thing. But that I have to keep an eye on him, that change can be dangerous, and he just had a sudden unpredictable change. I'm gonna write that he's back in the weeds.

ZEKE. Sounds about right.

BOBBY. Looking forward to seeing your fish tank, Zeke.

*(**ZEKE** laughs. **BOBBY**, about to leave, shakes **ZEKE**'s hand which turns into a hug.)*

ZEKE. Would you have cleaned those vents?

BOBBY. *(after a moment)* No, no I wouldn't have.

*(**BOBBY** leaves.)*

(lights down)

(end scene)

Scene III

(It is around two in the morning. JENNY, a very thin nineteen year-old girl, and ZEKE, carrying a shopping bag, have just arrived at his apartment. They are both a little drunk – JENNY a bit more so. ZEKE goes to the refrigerator and gets a couple of beers.)

ZEKE. Surprised you came home with me.

JENNY. Weren't you aiming to take me home?

(ZEKE gives JENNY a beer.)

ZEKE. Just aiming for a phone number.

JENNY. You're a better shot than you realized.

(ZEKE laughs. He puts his bag to the side.)

What's in there, anything exciting? Maybe some colored condoms – extra large of course.

ZEKE. *(laughing)* Just a dust buster.

JENNY. How dull.

(ZEKE puts on music.)

ZEKE. I never asked what you're in school for?

JENNY. Sex.

(ZEKE chokes on his beer, nearly spitting it out.)

I'm doing very well at it. Top of my class.

ZEKE. Don't remember that one on the curriculum. Must be a graduate school course.

JENNY. I'm only a freshman.

ZEKE. *(startled)* Freshman?

JENNY. Do I look older? Never tell a girl she looks older. Fashion. I'm at The New School for fashion. And how about you, any college?

ZEKE. Two years at SUNY Binghamton.

JENNY. Isn't that a four year…

ZEKE. I didn't exactly excel.

JENNY. All right, Zeke's a wild man.

ZEKE. *(laughing)* I'm planning on going back, becoming a teacher, high school teacher, working with the screwed up kids.

JENNY. That's noble of you. My man, Zeke is a noble man. And what's stopping your quest?

ZEKE. School's a little expensive right now.

You probably know all about that.

JENNY. My father takes care of it – about the only thing he's good for. He is not a noble man – he really dragged my mother over the coals in their divorce.

(raising her beer)

A toast, Zeke – to nobility.

(They toast and drink, and **JENNY** *slides right in next to* **ZEKE.***)*

I want to share my college education with you.

*(***JENNY** *kisses* **ZEKE.** *After a few moments, he pulls away.)*

Is something wrong?

(They hold each other's stare.)

Is there a problem?

ZEKE. *(getting up)* It's not suppose to go like this.

JENNY. What does that mean?

ZEKE. Why'd you come home with me?

JENNY. You invited me….

ZEKE. I just whisper a few sweet words…

JENNY. I thought we had a connection.

ZEKE. Do you do this a lot? Go home with a guy you just connected with?

JENNY. You're a breath away from calling me a slut, aren't you, Zeke?

ZEKE. *(after a moment)* With all you got going for you, I don't get it…

JENNY. Are you trying to open my eyes? Well, cut the bullshit, I'm not one of your screwed up students to be. You think cause I come from money, my life's a carnival? Everyone's messed up, just in different ways.

ZEKE. How does your dad feel about your messed up ways?

(pause)

JENNY. You were different at the bar – more lighthearted, charming.

You came over and offered to buy me a cheeseburger. No one's offered to buy me a cheeseburger before.

We were two people having fun – it felt good.

ZEKE. It did feel good.

New experiences, new possibilities

JENNY. That's right.

Why would you ruin that?

(no response)

Do I not measure up, Zeke, is that the problem? The alcohol's wearing off and you're wondering why the hell you invited this crazy girl home?

ZEKE. You measure up fine.

JENNY. Then what happened between here and the bar? What's wrong with me?

(no response)

If you're still wondering, I haven't been with a guy in over a year. I didn't think I was ready.

ZEKE. Now you do?

JENNY. I'm not so sure anymore.

(after a moment)

I'm gonna take off, if you decide I'm worthy, maybe we can try again some other time. Here's my number.

(pulls a pen and paper out of her purse)

If you call, make sure it's that guy I met in the bar. If not, well, have a nice life, and good luck with the school thing.

(She gives him her number. She goes to leave.)

ZEKE. Don't go, Jenny.

JENNY. Why not?

(JENNY *stops.*)

ZEKE. *(after a moment)* I know your old man.

JENNY. What? You know dear old Martin?

ZEKE. I used to work at the Essex House.

JENNY. And you think he's a great guy, right? Everyone thinks he's so wonderful, cause he's always throwing his money around. Well, he's a real shit, all right?

ZEKE. I agree.

JENNY. You do?

I guess we have something in common.

ZEKE. *(after a moment)* He got me fired.

JENNY. Fired? Why?

ZEKE. Dust. He wanted me to clean some dust.

JENNY. And you said no?

ZEKE. I did.

JENNY. Must have really pissed him off.

(JENNY *laughs and then stops, realizing her situation.*)

You knew I was his daughter before we met?

(no response)

I mean, I never told you my last name; how could you…

ZEKE. I saw the two of you having lunch at Le Cirque.

JENNY. *(after a moment)* Should I be worried?

(no response)

(getting scared) Listen, I'm outta here…

(JENNY *goes to leave.* ZEKE *stands in her way.*)

ZEKE. You're not going.

(JENNY *takes a step back.*)

JENNY. *(after a moment)* Why were you so concerned about me, about what I do?

ZEKE. Forgot who you were for a minute…

JENNY. Just thought I was some lost girl…

ZEKE. I guess so…

JENNY. But now you're back on track…

ZEKE. He shouldn't have done it…

JENNY. Stay away from me…

ZEKE. Sit down…

JENNY. Stay the hell away!

ZEKE. Sit the fuck down!

> *(pause)*

> (**JENNY** *sits on the edge of the futon.*)

JENNY. What are you going to do?

ZEKE. I don't know.
I didn't think you'd be here.

> *(pause)*

JENNY. I'm not him…

ZEKE. He was wrong…

JENNY. We're different…

ZEKE. He treated me like a fucking monkey!

> (**ZEKE** *slams his hand down on the table. It makes a booming sound.*)

> *(disbelief)* Dust, fucking dust…

JENNY. What the hell do you want from me?!
I'm leaving…

> (**ZEKE** *stares at her, stopping her in her tracks.*)

> *(quiet)* Can I go, Zeke?

> *(no response)*

> Are you going to hurt me to get even?

> *(no response)*

> *(quiet)* Are you going to hurt me?

ZEKE. *(after a moment)* No, I'm not gonna hurt you.

> (*After a moment,* **ZEKE** *gets the dust buster.*)

> I want you to give him this.

JENNY. The dust buster?

ZEKE. That's right.

    (**JENNY** *lets a laugh slip out.*)

    Give him this. Tell him you met me, what happened tonight.

    (*She takes it from him.*)

    Tell him it's not over.

JENNY. All right.

ZEKE. You can go.

    (**JENNY** *goes to leave and stops at the door.*)

JENNY. What are you gonna do?

ZEKE. He'll find out.

JENNY. This is a new experience – I was never so scared.

ZEKE. Run away, Jenny.

JENNY. You wouldn't hurt me. You're not built like that.

    (**JENNY** *and* **ZEKE** *hold each other's stare.*)

    You're like a gladiator, aren't you, Zeke? That nobility we toasted to…

ZEKE. You should stay away from me, far away. Nothing good can happen knowing me.

JENNY. Why did you invite me here?

    (*no response*)

    Was it only to put fear into my father?

ZEKE. (*after a moment – quiet*) I didn't want the night to end.

JENNY. It doesn't have to.

ZEKE. It already has.

    (*pause*)

JENNY. I'm sorry he hurt you.

ZEKE. What are you gonna tell him?

JENNY. That it's not over.

    (*After a moment,* **JENNY** *exits.*)

    (*After a moment,* **ZEKE** *sits down and his head falls in his hands.*)

    (*lights down*)

    (*end scene*)

Scene IV

(It is the morning. MARTIN *and* RALPH, *a large man in his late thirties, are in* MARTIN*'s apartment.)*

MARTIN. He wants to play games.

RALPH. He's definitely rolling the dice.

MARTIN. I'm sure he's planning something else.

RALPH. We won't let those plans occur.

MARTIN. No, no we won't.

Do we go to the police?

RALPH. If we prove it was him, that'd be a parole violation, he'd end up back in jail...

MARTIN. Jail sounds good, where he belongs...

RALPH. But it might be tough to prove.

MARTIN. Then we handle this ourselves.

RALPH. That's right, we handle this ourselves.

MARTIN. *(after a moment)* I came close to doing that in the gym. When I slammed my hand down on his table, I almost thought we were going to go at it. You know, hand to hand, man to man.

RALPH. That might not have turned out too good.

MARTIN. But it felt good. Made me feel young, powerful.

I started wondering if that made me a bit quick on the trigger, if I did the right thing.

RALPH. But now you know.

MARTIN. Yeah, now I know.

RALPH. A person like that isn't someone you want around.

MARTIN. What he did, that changes everything.

(after a moment)

The thought of him waking up with a smug smile etched on his face...

RALPH. Makes you wanna puke.

MARTIN. I want to do something, something....

RALPH. Devastating?

MARTIN. Yeah, devastating.

RALPH. You sure you want to push it that far?

MARTIN. He's come at me, destroying my property like he's spitting in my face.

(after a moment)

How about you, Ralph? This situation's different from one's in the past. How far are you willing to go?

RALPH. Whatever's necessary.

MARTIN. Suppose it requires…

RALPH. *(winking)* I've been in the trenches…

MARTIN. I know what happened to you overseas…

RALPH. Nothing that changed me.

I do what I do because I can, and I'm well paid to do it, very well paid when I work for you…

MARTIN. I respect who you are…

RALPH. Right back at you, big guy.

I do what I do because not many people are willing to get dirty.

Too many people talk – talking is dangerous at a time when action is necessary.

MARTIN. You're a tough S.O.B.

RALPH. Only when I need to be. Otherwise, I'm a great lover.

(MARTIN laughs.)

MARTIN. *(after a moment)* So let's take action.

The idea of breaking his parole, that's a keeper.

RALPH. We could plant some stolen goods in his apartment, right out in the open, and place an anonymous tip….

MARTIN. Good…

RALPH. *(snaps his fingers)* Presto, he's back on the chain gang.

MARTIN. That's very creative, Ralph.

RALPH. Better than the two of you lacing up the gloves.

(MARTIN *laughs.*)

MARTIN. That bastard wants to disrespect me, threaten me, destroy my property – he doesn't know who he's playing against.

(JENNY *enters the apartment. She will be even more sarcastic and flippant than usual, this is the case whenever she's around her father.*)

JENNY. Hello, Father. How are you this morning?

MARTIN. This is unexpected.

JENNY. I miss my dad.

MARTIN. I wish that were the truth.

JENNY. I've been doing a lot of thinking, and I've been talking to my therapist about you, and I finally realize what a remarkable man you are.

MARTIN. If that were the case, I'd double your shrink's salary.

(MARTIN *laughs.* JENNY *stays silent.*)

Should I have Ralph leave? I get the feeling a storm's brewing.

JENNY. Ralph can stay.

(*as if talking to a dog*)

Stay, Ralphy, stay – that's a good boy.

RALPH. (*like a dog*) Ruff, ruff…

JENNY. Oh, Ralphy likes to play…

MARTIN. Why don't I take you to dinner tonight, we'll have this conversation then.

JENNY. Is Daddy busy?

MARTIN. Yes, a bit busy.

JENNY. I won't be hungry.

Lunch once a week is all I can stomach.

MARTIN. (*after a moment*) Ralph, can you give us a few…

JENNY. Why is it that you're here, Ralphy? Daddy hasn't needed a bodyguard in a long time.

RALPH. For my charming personality.

JENNY. Daddy, have you not been playing nice on the play ground again? What did I tell you about that?

MARTIN. Damn it, Jenny...

JENNY. *(to* **RALPH***)* It is nice to know your by his side, to protect him from all those nasty bullies.

You know, Ralphy, I just might be hungry if you want to take me out...

MARTIN. Stop it! Stop this crap right now.

JENNY. Am I not good enough for Ralphy? Ralphy, do you not find me attractive?

RALPH. You're a lovely little crumpet.

JENNY. But I'm too fat, aren't I, Daddy?

MARTIN. I wish you could see what a beautiful woman you are.

JENNY. I wish so too.

(pause)

MARTIN. Why are you here?

JENNY. Torturing you isn't a good enough reason?

(no response)

I got you a present, Daddy.

(JENNY *reaches into her backpack and pulls out the dust buster.* **MARTIN** *stares at in disbelief.)*

MARTIN. What's that?

JENNY. A dust buster.

(JENNY *gives it to her father.)*

MARTIN. Why are you giving me this?

JENNY. It's good for cleaning dust.

MARTIN. Where did you get it?

JENNY. They're sold all over the place, but this particular model came from K-mart...

MARTIN. What the hell is going on?!

(no response)

RALPH. Tell us what happened, Jenny.

JENNY. *(after a moment)* Daddy had a man fired? Zeke Catchman?

MARTIN. How do you know that...

RALPH. He was disrespectful.

JENNY. *(to MARTIN)* Tell me more than that.

(no response)

Did he not wipe your ass when you were done taking a dump?

MARTIN. Watch your mouth...

JENNY. Explain to me how he was disrespectful; why you would mess with a man's life?

Maybe you're jealous because he's a strapping young lad, and with all your money it can't buy you health, can't buy you looks?

RALPH. But it can get you some good looking women.

JENNY. This is true. Daddy's never had trouble getting the women, have you, Daddy?

MARTIN. You don't know what you're...

JENNY. So you finally go to the gym, because the doctor tells you wine and steak isn't the breakfast of champions, and you pick a fight with an employee? I don't think that was the workout he had in mind.

MARTIN. It's not your concern.

JENNY. *(serious)* I keep hoping one day you'll be a man I can respect.

MARTIN. I hope so too, Jenny. I've told you I screwed up as a father...

JENNY. And a husband.

MARTIN. And maybe one day you'll let me make that up to you – there's nothing I wouldn't do for you.

Now you tell us.

JENNY. He gave me that dust buster to give to you.

RALPH. He's already given us one.

MARTIN. He smashed the window of my car, left it sitting on the front seat.

JENNY. At least he made it easy to clean up the broken glass.
I met your friend, Zeke, when I was at a bar, the Tenth
Street Lounge. I was drinking too much, and he invited
me back to his place. I went with him…

MARTIN. What are you thinking…

JENNY. Sorry to tell you, dear old Dad, but I'm not a virgin…

MARTIN. He's dangerous, a dangerous man, how could you
risk your life…

JENNY. What makes him so dangerous…

MARTIN. He's an ex-con!

JENNY. He never mentioned that. Not too many girls would
fall for that opening.

(after a moment)

What did he get arrested for?

RALPH. Burglary. He spent a year in Sing-Sing.

JENNY. In Ossining?

RALPH. That's right.

JENNY. So he had a place in Westchester? Maybe he's doing
better than I thought.

RALPH. He's also been arrested for beating a man…

MARTIN. Beating him near to death.

JENNY. So you're telling me he's a bad seed?

(pause)

MARTIN. Did he harm you in any way?

JENNY. In any way I didn't want you mean.

MARTIN. Stop it, Jenny.
Please, just tell me the truth.

JENNY. *(after a moment – serious)* Yes, he got violent. Yes, he
threw me around his apartment.
I'm scared. I'm terrified! He was out of control as he
towered over me, as he tossed me around, all because
of you, you and your macho fucking ego!

MARTIN. *(after a moment)* Are you all right?

(no response)

Did he…Did he…

JENNY. Sexually assault me?

MARTIN. Yes.

JENNY. No, he was a perfect gentleman.

He told me if you go to the police, he'll kill me.

(pause)

MARTIN. I'm going to put an end to this.

JENNY. How?

MARTIN. I'll take care...

JENNY. No, you won't! You won't be able to end it so easy.

He gave me one more message – that it's not over, that it's far from over.

(Pause, as JENNY and MARTIN stare at each other.)

Good-bye, Daddy. We'll do lunch next Thursday.

(JENNY goes to leave.)

MARTIN. Jenny.

(JENNY stops.)

I love you, Jenny.

JENNY. That's nice.

Now be careful when you sit in your car, you don't want any slivers of broken glass going up your ass.

(JENNY exits.)

MARTIN. He wants to hurt my daughter, threaten her life? Now he's gonna pay, now we throw him off the Brooklyn fucking Bridge!

RALPH. It doesn't add up. He threatens to kill her, and she goes dancing off into the sunset?

MARTIN. What are you saying?

RALPH. She's not telling you what really happened; she's riling you up. And doing a good job of it.

MARTIN. (after a moment – laughing) She's a bit eccentric, my daughter.

RALPH. (sarcastic) Hadn't noticed.

MARTIN. You don't have any kids do you, Ralph?

RALPH. I use protection.

MARTIN. I won't bore you by telling you how wonderful it once was, but it was wonderful. Things just get complicated…

I'd bust my ass working late, and when I'd come home Emily would be there freaking out, accusing me of cheating.

RALPH. *(sarcastic)* Yeah, sure working late, and I bet you stayed sometimes to catch up on your charity work.

MARTIN. Maybe I went out drinking with the boys a few times. Maybe I knew that'd piss her off. And she would get nasty, down right mean.

It got to the point where I did cheat on her. It felt good being around someone you wanted to be around.

(quiet) Yeah, If I could go back, I'd do some things differently.

(pause)

Is she in danger? Is Jenny in danger from this nut job?

RALPH. She knows him, and from his history you get the feeling he'd pick a fight with the Pope. So, yes, she's in danger.

(pause)

MARTIN. That son of a bitch has taken all the fun out of it involving my daughter.

It's time I stopped wasting my efforts, time to erase him from my life. I'll make a few phone calls, get him a handyman position at a different hotel. That'll make us even…

RALPH. Maybe he doesn't want a job, to be even.

Maybe revenge is consuming him.

MARTIN. He'll take any God damn thing that I offer.

RALPH. So we gonna put a horse's head in his bed?

MARTIN. He cannot get near my daughter. It ends now or it gets ugly.

(lights down)

(end scene)

Scene V

(**BOBBY** *has just arrived at* **ZEKE** *'s apartment.* **ZEKE** *has been writing and on a table is a pen, paper, and a few crumbled up balls of paper.* **BOBBY** *is holding a small fish bowl with a couple of fish in it.*)

BOBBY. Beginning of the kingdom.

(**BOBBY** *gives* **ZEKE** *the fish bowl which he places down.*)

Got you a butterfly fish cause he's a colorful sucker and a catfish. Everyone needs a catfish, they clean up all the garbage.

Food also.

(**BOBBY** *takes a container of fish food out of his pocket and places it down.*)

ZEKE. I appreciate it.

BOBBY. I appreciate your seeing me before our scheduled meeting.

ZEKE. You said it was important.

BOBBY. *(after a moment)* How you making out with the job search. What happened with Linda?

ZEKE. She thinks a lot of you, said you've been a great influence on her brother.

BOBBY. That's nice to hear.

ZEKE. You making sure I went?

BOBBY. I knew you'd go. I know you want to work.

ZEKE. She said nothing's available.

It was just a little overtime, trying to save a few coins for school...

BOBBY. All you need is one...

ZEKE. Everyone telling me no jobs are available...

BOBBY. One person to say yes...

ZEKE. Not a lot of people hiring ex-cons.

BOBBY. You have to be patient, it'll happen.

ZEKE. That's what she said. You speak with her?

BOBBY. Just to give a push in your direction.

Said she'd slide your application to the top of the pile.

ZEKE. Right.

(pause)

So why are you really here, Bobby?

(BOBBY *looks at the table where the writing is.)*

BOBBY. You doing a little writing?

ZEKE. Just a letter. Girl I met.

BOBBY. Good looking?

ZEKE. Yeah, definitely. She's hot.

BOBBY. Tell her that.

ZEKE. What?

BOBBY. That she's hot. Women always like to hear how good they look.

(ZEKE laughs.)

ZEKE. She's too young for me. She's young and confused, and I just want to share a few thoughts with her. Just want to remind her about what's important.

BOBBY. Easy to lose sight of.

I agree with you, Zeke, you'll be an excellent teacher, coach.

(pause)

ZEKE. What is it you want, Bobby?

BOBBY. I know you didn't get that job, and that lack of structure…

I haven't been exactly honest with you.

ZEKE. About what?

BOBBY. *(after a moment)* One of the steps…

ZEKE. Don't start this again…

BOBBY. The twelfth step actually…

ZEKE. I've got enough…

BOBBY. The twelfth step is to help others who have the disease.

I have to honor that step.

ZEKE. You do?

BOBBY. I didn't want you to know. Part of my job is to be a role model, but...

ZEKE. You were messed up?

BOBBY. I had a drinking problem. Almost cost me my marriage.

ZEKE. It cost me Rachel

BOBBY. You needed help. Without it, I never would have had Bobby Jr.

I have a great life, Zeke. I feel blessed every morning.

(pause)

I'm going to a meeting tonight. I want you to come as my guest. You won't have to say anything...

ZEKE. I don't need AA or NA...

BOBBY. You can just listen, hear the good...

ZEKE. I need that bastard to pay for fucking me up!

(pause)

BOBBY. Yeah, it's easy to lose sight of what's important.

(no response)

He didn't fuck you up.

You took care of that long before you met him.

ZEKE. Then why am I seeing his beady little eyes every time I get rejected?

BOBBY. You haven't taken responsibility...

ZEKE. You really believe this crap?

(pause)

BOBBY. It's like a baseball team, like our team. Sure you were the star, but when the three and five hitters started stroking the ball you got better pitches to hit, your job got a lot easier. The people around you, they can make you better. Like that letter you're writing.

(after a moment)

Come with me tonight.

ZEKE. Not gonna happen…

BOBBY. You can't do it alone…

ZEKE. I was doing fine, everything was falling into place…

BOBBY. I've been there…

ZEKE. Now I can't even afford my goddamn fish tank…

BOBBY. It's too fucking hard!

(pause)

(quiet) It's too hard to do alone.

ZEKE. I guess we'll find out.

BOBBY. Don't do anything stupid.

ZEKE. I'll see you next week.

*(**ZEKE** sits down and starts working on the letter. **BOBBY** goes to leave.)*

*(**BOBBY** stops.)*

BOBBY. *(after a moment)* What letter would you write yourself, Zeke?

ZEKE. You have a meeting to attend.

*(After a moment, **BOBBY** leaves.)*

*(After a moment, **ZEKE** continues working on the letter, as the lights slowly come down.)*

(end scene)

Scene VI

(It is late at night and the sounds of the city are heard. **ZEKE** *comes on stage and goes off to the side, to the shadows of an empty street.* **ZEKE** *is looking, waiting, stalking his prey.)*

(A man enters. He is looking for **ZEKE** *but doesn't see him.)*

(The man turns his back on **ZEKE** *and starts walking away.)*

*(***ZEKE** *springs on him from behind, but the man, sensing danger, turns just in time to catch* **ZEKE** *and toss him to the side.)*

(They spring back into action, as **ZEKE** *quickly gets to his feet, as the man starts to pull out his gun…)*

ZEKE. *(like a wild animal)* aaahhh…

*(***ZEKE** *leaps on him again, sending the gun skittering across the floor…)*

(They have a hold of each other, with neither having the upper hand – two animals, grunting and growling, fighting to survive…)

(blackout)

(end scene)

Scene VII

*(**MARTIN***'s apartment late at night.* **MARTIN** *enters and turns on the lights.* **ZEKE** *is sitting in a chair waiting for him.)*

ZEKE. Getting home late…

MARTIN. Jesus…

*(**ZEKE** stands.)*

ZEKE. How was dinner…

MARTIN. What the hell…

ZEKE. Cafe Carlyle makes for a nice date…

MARTIN. You're in deep shit!

ZEKE. Shut-up, Martin.

Now sit down before I knock you down.

(No one moves.)

Sit down!

(After a moment, **MARTIN** *does.)*

That's a nice looking woman you were dining with. Why didn't she come home with you? I was worried she might.

MARTIN. It was a first date.

ZEKE. Figured a stud like you beds 'em right away.

Maybe you forgot to take your Viagra, doubted your ability to perform.

*(**ZEKE** flips a vial of pills at* **MARTIN**.*)*

MARTIN. You went through my things?

ZEKE. Does that stuff make you good for two, three times a night, even at your age?

(no response)

Come on, Martin, I want to know what I have to look forward to, if I live that long.

(pause)

MARTIN. How did you get in?

ZEKE. I worked here for over six months, you don't think I
have a few connections with the housekeepers?

MARTIN. A housekeeper let you in?

ZEKE. Can't give you a name. I know the penchant you
have for helping people join the unemployment line.
I've been looking for work, but things are pretty dismal
out there...

MARTIN. You should have cleaned the damn vents!

ZEKE. Every time I get turned away, I think of you.
Every time I take a twenty out of a bank machine, I
think of you. Every fucking time I think about all the
strategies, dreams in my damn head looking so distant,
I think of you.

(pause)

MARTIN. What is it you want?

ZEKE. To get even.

MARTIN. How?

ZEKE. I might kill you.

MARTIN. You're going to kill me?

ZEKE. Ashes to ashes and dust to dust – isn't that how we
got here?

(ZEKE takes a gun out of his pants.)

You recognize this?

(no response)

Your friend had it on him, the one who was following
me last night...

MARTIN. I don't know...

ZEKE. You do...

MARTIN. Following you?...

ZEKE. I've seen you with him!
I've done some following of my own.
He thought he had an advantage, that he had no wor-
ries, but things aren't always so clear; it's hard to tell
where the danger lies.

(pause)

MARTIN. He was just suppose to talk with you…

ZEKE. Talk with me?

MARTIN. That's right.

ZEKE. Then why didn't he call?

(no response)

Why didn't you call?

MARTIN. It was to be done in a forceful manner.

ZEKE. To get your point across…

MARTIN. No harm was to come…

ZEKE. Just a bullet in the back.

MARTIN. *(after a moment)* He was to offer you a job.

ZEKE. You need a gun for that?

MARTIN. He was to insist that you take it. To tell you things were even between us, but that if you continue in your vehemence, things would get ugly.

ZEKE. Things are definitely ugly.

MARTIN. That's all that was suppose to happen.

(pause)

ZEKE. How is he?

MARTIN. A few broken ribs, busted nose, nothing much more than that.

ZEKE. That's good.

MARTIN. Do you want a job?

(no response)

Let things end between us?

ZEKE. That's not possible…

MARTIN. Why not?

ZEKE. 'Cause I'd have to trust you…

MARTIN. What the hell was I suppose to do?! I understood your message, sending my daughter here with that damn dust buster – that you could get at me in ways I couldn't even imagine, create pain I couldn't stand…

ZEKE. You should have fucking called!

MARTIN. *(after a moment)* Yes, yes maybe I should have. Do you want the job, let things end?

(no response)

It'll get you back on track.

ZEKE. *(after a moment)* Stand up.

(no response)

(forceful) Stand up.

(**MARTIN** *does.*)

Start hopping up and down.

MARTIN. What?

ZEKE. Start hopping…

MARTIN. I'm not…

ZEKE. Now! You start hopping…

(**ZEKE** *raises the gun…*)

(**MARTIN** *starts hopping.*)

That's good…

MARTIN. What's the point?

ZEKE. Higher. I want you jumping higher.

(**MARTIN** *starts jumping higher.*)

You keep a clean apartment, not a speck of dust anywhere.

(**MARTIN** *continues jumping.*)

You must be using the presents I got you.

(after a few moments)

You can stop.

(**MARTIN** *does. He is out of breath.*)

MARTIN. Let me get you a job. I know some people at the Carlyle, I've already talked to them, they need someone…

ZEKE. Shut the hell up!

MARTIN. *(after a moment)* I was wrong. I admit it.

I didn't want to be there, hadn't been to a gym in like five years. I saw my doctor the day before, he said bad things about my health, my heart – he has me on all these damn pills...

I can't stand the thought that I'm fading away, that my time's running out.

ZEKE. That doesn't...

MARTIN. It's like I'm a carton of milk going sour, like I can see the expiration date on my birth certificate. That's why I was so quick tempered.

ZEKE. Jumping Jacks.

MARTIN. I'm sorry, Zeke. I was out of line...

ZEKE. Start jumping!

MARTIN. Oh, shit.

(MARTIN starts doing jumping jacks.)

(ZEKE is pacing the room, trying to stay calm.)

ZEKE. I almost feel like making you suck my dick.

(MARTIN is doing jumping jacks.)

(after a few moments)

Five more and you can stop. Count 'em out.

(MARTIN counts out five and stops. He is winded.)

How do you like being the dog?

(No response.)

How do you...

MARTIN. I don't!

ZEKE. Didn't think you would.

Now tell me...

MARTIN. What?! What the hell do you want me to tell you?!

ZEKE. How you got like this?

MARTIN. The doctor...

(ZEKE raises the gun.)

Don't, do it, Zeke...

ZEKE. Why you did that to me…

(*ZEKE has the gun pointed at* **MARTIN** *and walks towards him.*)

MARTIN. I was wrong; I'm sorry…

(*ZEKE now has the gun pressed against* **MARTIN***'s forehead…*)

ZEKE. It doesn't make any damn sense…

MARTIN. Both our lives end with that trigger…

(*ZEKE punches* **MARTIN** *in the face. He goes down…*)

ZEKE. It was dust, just fucking dust!

(*ZEKE hits* **MARTIN** *again and again.* **MARTIN** *is curled up on his side covering up.* **ZEKE***'s fist is cocked to strike once more, but he doesn't. He places the gun against* **MARTIN***'s head.*)

(*A moment – will he kill him?*)

(*ZEKE lets go.*)

(*ZEKE stands and takes a step back. He is trying his best to control his rage.*)

(*After a moment,* **ZEKE** *goes to leave but stops.*)

ZEKE. If you try and retaliate, if you go to the police, someone dies, someone definitely dies.

(*ZEKE leaves the apartment.*)

(*After a moment,* **MARTIN** *tries to get up, but he collapses.*)

(*He tries again and is able to rise.*)

(*On wobbly legs, he slowly walks to the chair and sits.*)

(*He takes a handkerchief out of his pocket, places it on his nose to stop the bleeding, and tilts his head back.*)

(*The lights slowly come down.*)

(*end scene*)

ACT II

Scene I

(It is the next night. **ZEKE** *has just arrived at* **DIGS**' *apartment.* **DIGS** *is a black man in his late twenties.)*

DIGS. Zeke, my man! What's up, yo?

ZEKE. Good to see you, Digs.

(They shake hands and it turns into a hug.)

DIGS. Look at you, bro, musta put on twenty pounds.

ZEKE. It's my special pizza diet.

*(***DIGS*** laughs.)*

DIGS. Sit the fuck down, let me get you a beer.

*(***DIGS*** gets two beers and gives one to* **ZEKE**.*)*

What brings you up here?

ZEKE. Coming to see if you got any uglier.

DIGS. You know why I like getting up in the morning? 'Cause I get prettier every day.

*(***DIGS*** laughs.)*

Wasn't you on the inside?

ZEKE. Twelve months – Sing-sing.

DIGS. Tough place.

ZEKE. Wouldn't want to vacation there.

DIGS. Ain't you breaking the rules coming to see me, known felon and all?

ZEKE. I won't say nothing, if you don't.

*(***DIGS*** laughs.)*

DIGS. *(after a moment – serious)* It's good to see you, Z, but you should take off.

43

ZEKE. You worried about me?

DIGS. Worried who you might be working for.

ZEKE. It's not like that...

DIGS. How many they tell you to get...

ZEKE. I'm cool...

DIGS. Don't bullshit me, dog!

They let you out to nark on a few – friends being the easy mark...

(**ZEKE** *pulls out his gun.*)

What's up with that, yo? What the fuck is that?!

(*no response*)

(*disbelief*) You robbing me, Z?

ZEKE. Letting you know which side I'm playing on. If I'm working for the law, I wouldn't be carrying no piece.

DIGS. I guess you wouldn't.

(*after a moment*) Let me see it.

(**ZEKE** *hands* **DIGS** *the gun.*)

I'll put it over here.

(**DIGS** *places the gun near him and away from* **ZEKE.**)

You having a piece makes me nervous. You got a track record for busting up dealers.

ZEKE. Just one.

DIGS. (*laughing*) Little Mo, dusted him pretty good.

ZEKE. Tried selling me fake dope.

DIGS. Fucking Mo was in the hospital for like two weeks. He's a punk ass anyway.

Mind if I do a little inspection?

(**ZEKE** *stands and raises his arms.* **DIGS** *frisks him.*)

ZEKE. You think I'd take you down, Digs?

DIGS. A man would turn on his grandmother to save his skin.

Only one place left to look, and you best not get excited.

*(*DIGS *quickly grabs his crotch.)*

DIGS. *(cont.) (joking)* Not a bad package for a white man. You're cool, sit your ass back down.

You still smoke?

*(*DIGS *pulls out a bag of pot with a joint already rolled in it.)*

I know you straight now. You all chubby and clean looking. You're skin all shiny...

ZEKE. I could be on an Ivory soap commercial...

DIGS. Riding one of them horses.

*(*DIGS *laughs.)*

You wanna smoke a little? Just pot, no dust or nothing.

*(*DIGS *lights up the joint and takes a hit. He passes it to* **ZEKE**. **ZEKE** *just holds the joint.)*

You gonna hit it or what? Ain't no big thing.

(After a moment, **ZEKE** *takes a hit.)*

This is the good shit. My old dog Z comes to town, ain't gonna be cracking out no bunk.

ZEKE. Tastes good.

DIGS. Like mama's milk.

*(*ZEKE *takes another hit and passes the joint to* **DIGS**.)*

ZEKE. What's the gun worth?

DIGS. I ain't no arms dealer.

ZEKE. You could get something for it.

DIGS. *(checking out the gun)* Might keep it for myself, depending on what you want.

ZEKE. A couple grams; we'll say an eight-ball...

DIGS. Get outta here, dog; you clean now...

ZEKE. Got an edge to me...

DIGS. Don't be going back down that path...

ZEKE. I gotta find some peace.

DIGS. This "J" will give you some peace.

(**DIGS** *passes the joint to* **ZEKE**.)

Now tell me what's squeezing you?

ZEKE. Just missing the taste.

DIGS. This ain't no Juicy Fruit gum.

Yo, Z, we've gotten messed up passed the early hours of the morning, making sense out of shit that don't have no sense. You tell me what's going down, and we'll make sense out of it.

(no response)

A girl involved? Nothing turns a man into a ninety-eight pound weakling quicker than a woman who stops smiling at you.

ZEKE. *(after a moment)* I fucked up, Digs.

DIGS. We're men, fucking up is what we do.

ZEKE. I went to see my old girlfriend Rachel. She's living in this big house in the suburbs…

(**ZEKE** *stops talking.*)

DIGS. *(after a moment)* And she wasn't buying what you were selling?

ZEKE. Shows me her engagement ring.

DIGS. Ouch.

ZEKE. *(quiet)* This is my life now. Here with you.

DIGS. I am a sexy man.

Just take a breath my brother, take a breath. Things a man don't have always sound good…

ZEKE. That crank, that's what sounds good…

DIGS. With your romping stomping ways a house out in the suburbs would have been Sing-Sing revisited…

ZEKE. Fuck you, Digs, I don't need no counseling.

That bag, it'll last me a few nights, and then I'll go straight again.

DIGS. Ain't never seen that happen.

(pause)

ZEKE. We have a deal or not?

(no response)

I'll go elsewhere if you've joined the church choir.

DIGS. Z, look at me. Look at me, motherfucker.

(ZEKE does.)

You understand when this shit grabs you a second time, it's a vice grip, it's like that Kung-fu grip, it ain't letting go.

ZEKE. You gonna give me a pamphlet or something?

DIGS. *(after a moment)* All right, dog.

Eight-ball for the gun?

ZEKE. Need a pipe too.

(DIGS gets the bag.)

DIGS. Don't feel right, me laying this on you.

ZEKE. I can handle it.

DIGS. You've gotten yourself clean.

ZEKE. Maybe I ain't meant to be clean.

(After a moment, DIGS gives ZEKE the bag)

DIGS. *(joking)* This is the real shit, yo, so I don't want you coming back to stomp my ass.

(laughing) Fucking Little Mo.

(ZEKE opens the bag and examines the contents.)

ZEKE. It's cool. Pipe.

(DIGS gives ZEKE a pipe.)

DIGS. You sure you know what you're doing, playing with the devil and all?

(After a moment, ZEKE takes out the drugs, puts it in the pipe, and lights up. He takes a long hit.)

How you feeling, bro?

ZEKE. Like I'm back home. Feels good to be home.

DIGS. I hear you, dog.

(ZEKE takes another hit.)

(**ZEKE** *gets up and starts walking to the other side of the stage.* **DIGS** *watches him, as the lights slowly come down on* **DIGS**.)

(*Halfway there* **ZEKE** *stops and takes another hit.*)

(**ZEKE** *is now feeling good. He starts dancing around like a boxer, throwing some punches. He raises his arms in the air like he's just won a big fight. Yeah, he's definitely feeling good.*)

(*After a moment, he continues walking to his apartment. He sits on his futon.*)

(*After a moment, he curls up and goes to sleep.*)

(*The lights slowly come down.*)

(*end scene*)

Scene II

(It is the early evening of the next day. **JENNY** *has just arrived at* **ZEKE***'s apartment. She is wearing a short skirt, looking very attractive.* **ZEKE***, looking haggard, is still wearing what he had on from the night before.* **ZEKE** *has left his bag of drugs on the table next to the fish bowl. The futon is now open as a bed.)*

ZEKE. What are you doing here?

JENNY. Checking up on you.

ZEKE. I told you to stay away.

JENNY. I like you watching out for my best interest.

So you want the update on my father?

(no response)

I gave him the dust buster – he freaked when he saw it. Told me about the one you put in his car.

(laughing)

That was brilliant, truly brilliant. I also told him how you picked me up in a bar, how easy I was…

ZEKE. I don't need to hear this.

JENNY. I did it for you.

I rattled his cage for you.

ZEKE. It's over now, it doesn't matter.

JENNY. What did he do?

ZEKE. Nothing…

JENNY. Nothing? Then it's not over.

ZEKE. We had a talk…

JENNY. This is why I came by, to warn you, to make sure you don't underestimate him. He does not go gentle into that good night.

*(***ZEKE***, next to the fish bowl, secretively, puts the drugs in his pocket.)*

When did you get the fish? You don't seem like a fish kind of guy.

ZEKE. Why would you go against your own father?

JENNY. To watch him squirm.

When the fights were bad at home, and mom and I would be devastated, nothing ever seemed to affect him. He'd have this smirk on his face, this half-smile… I want to see him on the spit, roasting over the open fire. Not very lady like, is it?

(no response)

(in a pseudo **ZEKE** *voice)* Why yes, Jenny, you are very lady like, and you look ravishing tonight also.

(no response)

What's wrong, Zeke? You look so beat up, so unhappy. Is it because of this stuff with my…

ZEKE. No.

JENNY. Let me help you.

ZEKE. I appreciate the kindness, but you should leave.

JENNY. I want to return the kindness you showed me.

That letter means a lot to me.

(no response)

Why did you write it?

ZEKE. *(after a moment)* You asked what was wrong with you, it sounded like you always carry this thought in your hip pocket.

JENNY. So you wanted to open my eyes?

ZEKE. Remind you of things, yeah. You needed reminding.

JENNY. *(after a moment)* What do you need?

(no response)

Maybe you need to talk, to not keep everything bottled up.

You probably watched too many Clint Eastwood movies as a kid. He was always so tough, so macho, but he never seemed very happy.

ZEKE. Talking about feelings isn't my forte.

JENNY. What is?

ZEKE. Not talking about feelings.

JENNY. Try. Try telling me about all that shit inside of you.

(**ZEKE** *is about to say something, but he stops and laughs.*)

I know what it's like.

It's like your brain starts working and you can't shut it off, and you want to; you want to stop thinking, to stop feeling, but it doesn't seem possible.

Am I close at all?

(*no response*)

Tell me I'm way off, that I'm nutcase, and I'll leave.

ZEKE. (*after a moment*) No, you're not nuts.

JENNY. You almost talked, does it feel any better?

(**ZEKE** *laughs.*)

ZEKE. (*after a moment*) I want to be who I once was. I want to feel strong, like I can do anything, but... but...

JENNY. You get weaker everyday.

ZEKE. Yeah, weaker...

I don't know how to go about it.

JENNY. About what?

ZEKE. Stuff that should be easy. Like, you know, a girl, a house, family. I want that shit. But everyday it seems further away, and it's like I can't do anything to stop it, like everything's out of control...

(**ZEKE** *stops talking.*)

(*after a moment*) You should go...

JENNY. No, Zeke...

ZEKE. (*exploding*) Quit pushing me, God damn it! Would you quit pushing me?! Just get the hell out!

(*Pause, as they hold each other's stare.*)

(*quiet*) I'm not any good.

(**JENNY** *goes to* **ZEKE**, *who is sitting on the futon.*)

JENNY. "People don't see their own worth, their own greatness – I can see yours."

ZEKE. You memorized the letter? What about the part not
to contact me?

(JENNY *starts massaging* ZEKE*'s shoulders.*)

JENNY. "It radiates in your abundance of energy, in your
uniqueness of spirit."

ZEKE. I'm a different animal than you.
You think I'm somebody I'm not.

JENNY. I know what you are.

(JENNY *unbuttons his shirt.*)

(JENNY *takes* ZEKE*'s shirt off and lies him down on his
side, in the fetal position.*)

(*She gently rubs his back.*)

(*after a few moments*) "Don't fight against your greatness, believe in it and embrace it."

(ZEKE *rolls over and looks at her.*)

I love what you wrote.

(JENNY *gently gives* ZEKE *a kiss.*)

(*After a moment,* ZEKE *kisses* JENNY, *and they become
very passionate, undressing each other.*)

(*The lights slowly come down.*)

(*The lights come back up. It is a few hours later.*)

(ZEKE *is getting dressed, as* JENNY *lies in bed under the
covers.*)

ZEKE. Jenny.

(*no response*)

(*a little louder*) Jenny.

(*She's asleep.*)

(ZEKE *pulls the drugs out of his pocket and sees that he
is running low.*)

(*He stares at* JENNY *for a moment*)

(*He then goes to her pocketbook and takes out her wallet.
He helps himself to a couple of twenties. He puts the
wallet away.*)

(**ZEKE** *is on edge, thinking about getting stoned. He walks over to her and shakes her awake.*)

ZEKE. *(cont.)* Hey, Jenny, get up now.

JENNY. Hello, Zeke. You look better already.

ZEKE. You got to get up, get dressed.

JENNY. Can't we just lie around for a while? We could order in some Chinese food…

ZEKE. I have things to do.

JENNY. Aren't you hungry? I worked up quite an appetite…

ZEKE. *(snapping)* Get dressed, all right?

JENNY. Jesus…

(*After a moment,* **JENNY** *gets out of bed and starts getting dressed.*)

What's so urgent at this hour?

(*No response, as* **JENNY** *continues getting dressed.*)

I was thinking of getting breast implants, would you like that?

Poetry sex is great and all, but I think big breasts bring out the primordial thing.

(**JENNY** *comes up close to* **ZEKE**.)

They could be fun to play with.

(**JENNY** *starts kissing* **ZEKE**'s *neck.*)

ZEKE. *(backing away)* Cut it out, cut this shit out!

JENNY. Fuck you, Zeke! Why do you have to be so mean? We just had sex, shared something intense…I can't believe the way you're treating me!

ZEKE. *(sincere)* I'm sorry, Jenny. I'm sorry.

(*They hold each other's stare.*)

No, you don't need breast implants; you're a beautiful girl.

JENNY. Then why are you throwing me out?

ZEKE. I have things to take care of.

JENNY. Drugs?

ZEKE. *(after a moment)* No, not drugs.

JENNY. My father told me a lot about you.

I saw a bag on the table.

If you have a problem, that doesn't scare me…

ZEKE. Everything's under control.

(pause)

(JENNY has finished getting dressed.)

JENNY. Are you feeling any better?

ZEKE. I am.

JENNY. That's good.

(After a moment, JENNY goes to leave, but then she stops.)

You're the first man I've been with in a year.

ZEKE. Hope I didn't disappoint.

JENNY. You were a real stud.

(ZEKE laughs.)

Had my heart broke. I was in love, thought things were going great, and I made dinner for us one night, and he dumped me.

ZEKE. Things fall apart quickly.

JENNY. Maybe they come together quickly, when you find someone to connect with.

(after a moment)

I won't come by again, but if you call, I don't know, maybe something magical can happen. And if not magical, at least we could have some good sex. Nothing wrong with that, is there?

ZEKE. You're so young, Jenny.

JENNY. What does that mean?

ZEKE. You still believe everything's gonna work out in the end.

JENNY. And maybe it is. You haven't reached the end of your path, finished trotting along your yellow brick road.

ZEKE. Yeah, maybe I haven't.

(pause as they hold each other's stare)

JENNY. Thank you for the letter, Zeke Catchman.

*(After a moment, **JENNY** exits.)*

ZEKE. *(after a moment – quiet)* Jenny…

(He walks towards the door, but stops.)

(loud – angst) Jenny!

*(After a moment, **ZEKE** slams the door closed.)*

(lights down)

(end scene)

Scene III

(The stage will be split into two separate playing areas. There will be a "switch focus" stage direction to determine which side is in action.)

*(**RALPH** has just arrived over **MARTIN**'s apartment. **MARTIN**, unshaven for the first time in the play, is sporting a black eye and looks disheveled.)*

RALPH. Nice eye.

MARTIN. Right.

RALPH. *(joking)* Guess your date didn't go as well as you had hoped.

MARTIN. Zeke came here.

RALPH. I told you you needed protection.

MARTIN. He was sitting in that chair when I got home.

RALPH. A regular surprise party.

What did I say? That we had to take action after he kicked the crap out of Tyler, that he was a rabid dog waiting to pounce.

MARTIN. *(after a moment)* I came in, and he had a gun. Tyler's gun...

RALPH. That's a loud bark...

MARTIN. He placed it against my head; he wanted me to beg, beg for my life, for forgiveness.

RALPH. Did you?

MARTIN. No.

RALPH. That's good.

MARTIN. So he pummeled me.

RALPH. Let's see how that dog does begging...

MARTIN. I want to tear his damn limbs off, torture him to a slow fucking death!

RALPH. *(after a moment)* He's gotten the better of us, but I won't let that happen again, not a chance. Or I've been beaten, then I should be selling hotdogs at Nathans. Now it's our turn.

(SWITCH FOCUS)

(It is the early evening. ZEKE, *crashing from his high, and holding his motorcycle helmet, is with* BOBBY *on the patio at* BOBBY's *house. There are a couple of chairs and an outdoor chest.)*

ZEKE. Who takes care of the garden? Damn, the place is beautiful – never pictured you as a gardener, Bobby.

BOBBY. *(laughing)* The wife does most of it.

ZEKE. What are those flowering things?

BOBBY. She calls them Azaleas.

ZEKE. Nice.

(after a moment) You said if I ever felt the urge, I should call.

BOBBY. And you're feeling it?

ZEKE. A little more than that.

*(*ZEKE *looks* BOBBY *in the eyes for the first time.)*

BOBBY. You're all fucked up?

ZEKE. Yeah, I'm fucked.

(after a moment) I don't want to be here.

BOBBY. I'm glad you came by.

ZEKE. No where else to go.

BOBBY. You're alone. A person's not meant to be alone…

ZEKE. I'm crashing, Bobby, I'm crashing hard!

BOBBY. Take it easy, Zeke.

(After a moment, ZEKE *takes the twenties he stole from* JENNY *out of his pocket.)*

ZEKE. Look at this, at these twenties.

BOBBY. *(confused)* All right, I'm looking at 'em.

ZEKE. I stole them.

That girl, Jenny, the one I was writing the letter to. I liked her – she's different, unique…From Rachel, I stole them from Rachel.

BOBBY. What are you talking about…

ZEKE. When we were together, I took them, and that was the end of us…

(after a moment) I spend all my time thinking about what was, what I once had…

BOBBY. And nothing about what can be? You got to focus…

ZEKE. Nothing seems possible.

I think about high school, about Rachel, that being the best part of my life. I was only smoking a little weed, drinking a few beers…Everything was in control.

I think about our baseball team, winning the state championship…

BOBBY. We had a helluva team…

ZEKE. That can't be the highlight! That can't be.

(quiet) I'm too young to be thinking my best days are behind me.

(SWITCH FOCUS)

RALPH. I'll think of something, maybe not as colorful as torturing him to death, but something.

MARTIN. *(after a moment – quiet)* I'm not so sure.

RALPH. About what?

MARTIN. I can't make any rash decisions, let my emotions rule – the stakes are too high.

I have to think about the repercussions.

RALPH. There won't be any repercussions, I'll make sure of that.

MARTIN. *(quiet)* I have to think about what I'm capable of.

RALPH. That's what you said after Tyler…

MARTIN. Everything's out of fucking control!

(pause)

RALPH. When I was investing in the stock market, I followed your advice – for getting in, and, obviously, for getting out. I've done very well. You're now in my field of expertise, expertise that will save you, save your daughter.

Do you understand me, Martin?

MARTIN. My daughter.

RALPH. This is the time for action, no more thinking.

(SWTICH FOCUS)

*(***BOBBY*** *pulls two baseball mitts and a ball out of the outdoor chest.)*

BOBBY. *(cont.)* Put this on.

*(***BOBBY*** *offers* ***ZEKE*** *a mitt. After a moment of staring at it,* ***ZEKE*** *puts his helmet down and puts it on. He pounds the webbing)*

Feels good, doesn't it?

(No response.)

How long's it been?

ZEKE. *(quiet)* Don't know.

*(***BOBBY*** *steps back, throws the ball, and* ***ZEKE*** *catches it.* ***ZEKE*** *weighs the ball in his hand before throwing it back. They will play catch.)*

BOBBY. It was an awesome team. And you made me feel like I belonged, the way you worked with me on my hitting. Damn, I got a lot better.

(They play catch.)

You see kids playing catch and you want to be that young again, to go back, to have a chance at some different decisions – today, that's all possible.

ZEKE. You talk too much.

BOBBY. Wouldn't have to if you listened better.

(After a moment, ***ZEKE*** *throws the ball over* ***BOBBY****'s head on purpose.)*

What was that?

ZEKE. An error, Bobby, a fucking error.

*(***ZEKE*** *takes off the mitt and throws it at* ***BOBBY****'s feet.)*

(SWITCH FOCUS)

RALPH. You leave him alone and he'll return, he'll return just like that freak from Halloween.

MARTIN. How can you be so sure?

RALPH. Because rage doesn't disappear. Because he has nothing to live for and blames that on you.

(pause)

MARTIN. He had something.

RALPH. *(laughing)* A bullshit handy man job?

MARTIN. I shouldn't have gotten him fired...

RALPH. It's way beyond that...

MARTIN. Knew it was wrong when it was going down...

RALPH. He's beat you down...

MARTIN. But I was so damn angry about my health...

RALPH. Threatened your daughter...

MARTIN. I couldn't stop myself...

RALPH. You're not the one who needs stopping!

(pause)

MARTIN. I need some time, Ralph...

RALPH. No.

MARTIN. No?

RALPH. I listened to you once, things went badly; I won't let that happen again...

MARTIN. You're job is to do what I tell you...

RALPH. My job is to make sure everything works out correctly. My job is to not follow orders that demonstrate bad judgment.

A man has to protect his honor. A man has to protect his family.

What kind of man are you, Martin?

(no response)

What kind of man will you be when crazy Jenny isn't around to howl at the moon?

(SWITCH FOCUS)

ZEKE. *(attacking – sarcastic)* I know you were a lush, but you ever get stoned?

BOBBY. Not much.

ZEKE. Just a drunk loser, is that it?

BOBBY. *(confused)* What the hell are you…

ZEKE. I think you're bullshitting me, a black man not getting stoned, never heard of such a thing.

BOBBY. I know you're wasted, but don't…

ZEKE. Dude who sells me the crank is African-American…

BOBBY. Don't start with the racial…

ZEKE. Why do your people get all the good shit…

BOBBY. Shut your mouth…

ZEKE. *(in* **BOBBY***'s face)* I'm your nigger, nigger!

BOBBY. Shut your fucking mouth!

> *(***BOBBY*** grabs a handful of* **ZEKE***'s shirt.)*

ZEKE. You gonna give your nigger a beat down?

> *(After a moment,* **BOBBY** *lets go.)*

You gonna bring me in, cowboy?

> *(no response)*

I'm outta here…

> *(***ZEKE*** grabs his helmet and goes to leave.* **BOBBY** *grabs him again, to stop him.)*

BOBBY. I can't let you…

ZEKE. Get the fuck off!

> *(***ZEKE*** pushes* **BOBBY** *in the chest.* **BOBBY** *punches* **ZEKE** *in the face, sending him down.* **ZEKE** *springs up.)*

I'll tear you the fuck up!

> *(***ZEKE*** approaches.)*

> *(SWITCH FOCUS)*

MARTIN. The only way to stop him is to kill him?

RALPH. That's right.

MARTIN. You can do this?

RALPH. As easy as digging a hole.

You know I've been in the trenches.

MARTIN. Yes.

(*pause*)

RALPH. Only you and I can know about this, so you keep your mouth shut or it gets dangerous, or those repercussions you mentioned become a reality.

Do you understand?

MARTIN. (*quiet*) This is the time for action

RALPH. Action is necessary.

MARTIN. I have to protect my daughter.

RALPH. That's right.

MARTIN. Her life's dangling there.

RALPH. I'll put that dog to sleep.

(*pause*)

MARTIN. No, no, Ralph.

RALPH. What?

MARTIN. I can't do it.

RALPH. What kind of man are you?

MARTIN. I won't be needing your services any longer…

RALPH. What kind of fucking man are you?!

(*SWITCH FOCUS*)

BOBBY. Come on, Zeke, give your P.O. a beat down!

ZEKE. (*after a moment – quiet*) No, not you, can't jump at you.

BOBBY. What can you jump at, more meth?

(*no response*)

You got some on you? Come on, crack out the crank – I'll smoke it with you. Let me taste the bitch that owns you.

(*No response.*)

Crack out the crank!

(*After a moment, ZEKE takes out the drugs and pipe and puts some crank in it. He gives it to BOBBY.*)

(*Both sides of the stage will now be active with the speeches intertwining.*)

RALPH. He placed a gun against your head. He was a spasm away from ending your life.

(*RALPH's finger is pressed against* MARTIN's *head as though it were a gun*)

BOBBY. Need a lighter.

(*ZEKE hands* BOBBY *a lighter. They hold each other's stare.*)

MARTIN. I've thought about that, suppose a piece of dust floats in his nostril; he sneezes, jerks the trigger – how ironic that would be...

(**BOBBY** *lights the lighter.*)

RALPH. *(shooting his gun finger)* Boom! You'd be dead.

(**BOBBY** *puts the lighter to the bowl and starts to inhale.* ZEKE *suddenly smacks it out of his hand, sending the pipe and lighter flying...*)

ZEKE. What the fuck are you doing?! Did you get any of that shit in you...

MARTIN. You're going to leave it alone...

ZEKE. Answer me, God damn it!

BOBBY. You smacked it out of my hands before I could...

RALPH. He beat the shit out of Tyler...

MARTIN. Those are the risks that come with your occupation...

RALPH. I'm hunting him down!

ZEKE. Suppose I hadn't...

BOBBY. I'd have smoked, and you'd be back in prison...

RALPH. You're not the man I thought you were.

BOBBY. You wouldn't have been the man I thought you were.

(*pause*)

It's your choice now, Zeke.

MARTIN. That gun against my head, it's opened my eyes – how stupid I would be to risk everything in such a ridiculous fashion.

BOBBY. Sitting alone, there's no one to knock the pipe away.

(pause)

ZEKE. Before, what I said, I didn't mean…

BOBBY. I know.

MARTIN. I can never be the one holding the gun.

ZEKE. I'm not like that.

BOBBY. What are you like?

Why are you here?

(pause)

ZEKE. *(quiet)* You can't save me, Bobby.

RALPH. All you know about me, you know I'm not walking away.

ZEKE. After I did it, took those twenties from Rachel, I was able to do things, things I never thought I'd do – things a man doesn't do.

MARTIN. You hunt him down, and I'll testify against you.

ZEKE. I couldn't stop myself. I can't stop myself.

MARTIN. There will be repercussions.

ZEKE. I know how this ends up.

RALPH. You're gonna spend all your days thinking about what you could have done, should have done, but didn't do.

ZEKE. I know where I end up.

(pause)

BOBBY. Pick your pipe up off the ground. Isn't that what you need?

*(**ZEKE** doesn't move.)*

RALPH. You need my help and you're turning it down…

BOBBY. Let me help you…

*(**BOBBY** picks up the pipe and offers it to **ZEKE**.)*

MARTIN. I need nothing from you.

*(**ZEKE** takes hold of it, but **BOBBY** doesn't let go.)*

BOBBY. I have a great life now, Zeke…

MARTIN. Get out…

BOBBY. I feel blessed every day.

RALPH. You're gonna be a devastated man, Martin.

BOBBY. Why'd you smack it out of my hands?

(After a moment, **BOBBY** *lets go of the pipe and suddenly smacks it out of* **ZEKE** *'s hand…)*

MARTIN. I don't want to see you again…

BOBBY. We're even now…

MARTIN. Not even on a post office wall…

BOBBY. Now pick up your pipe and…

BOBBY/MARTIN. Get the fuck out!

(pause)

*(***ZEKE** *kneels down to pick up the pipe.)*

RALPH. *(after a moment)* Leaving you alive, killing young Jenny – that's pain, that's revenge.

(After a moment, **RALPH** *leaves.)*

*(***ZEKE,** *kneeling, is holding the pipe in his hand, weighing it like he did earlier with the baseball.)*

*(***BOBBY** *starts to walk away from* **ZEKE.** *)*

ZEKE. *(after a moment – quiet)* I need help.

*(***BOBBY** *stops and faces* **ZEKE.** *)*

BOBBY. What are you, Zeke?

ZEKE. *(anguish)* A fucking addict…

*(***ZEKE** *places the pipe on the ground and stands.)*

(long pause)

BOBBY. You got two choices – the better one is joining a program.

(no response)

*(***MARTIN** *goes to a drawer, takes out a case, and sits back down.)*

You won't be alone. Life's too difficult, too painful for a man alone.

We all need someone to smack the pipe away.

(**MARTIN** *opens the case and looks inside - it's a gun that the audience doesn't see.*)

(**ZEKE** *takes the drugs out of his pocket. He stares at it.*)

(*After a moment,* **ZEKE** *empties the drugs in his hands.*)

ZEKE. Am I still your nigger?

BOBBY. Always will be.

(**ZEKE** *blows the drugs away, as* **MARTIN** *slams shut his case.*)

(*lights down*)

(*end scene*)

Scene IV

(It is later that same day. ZEKE has just arrived at JENNY's one bedroom apartment. They are in the living room. JENNY has an edge to her.)

JENNY. Surprised you called, that you've come to my home.

ZEKE. Weren't you aiming to take me home?

JENNY. I was only aiming for meaningless sex.

ZEKE. You just might hit your target.

JENNY. *(cold)* I already have.

(They hold each other's stare.)

You look like a vagrant.

ZEKE. Thanks.

JENNY. Been out playing with drugs again?

(No response.)

Stupid question, right? It's like asking a fat person if they ate the missing brownie.

So why'd you come here, because I doubt your little fella is gonna be able to come out and play after a drug binge.

ZEKE. *(after a moment)* I owe you this.

(ZEKE takes the twenties out of his pocket.)

JENNY. Am I a whore, you want to pay for my services?

(no response)

Don't tell me, I'm so good you figure I have to be a pro...

ZEKE. It's yours...

JENNY. I don't know if I should be insulted or compli-mented.

ZEKE. I took it...

JENNY. I know you took it!

I wasn't asleep. I never sleep...

ZEKE. Here, you go...

JENNY. I don't want the damn money!

Here, you can dip your fingers in my Gucci wallet...

(JENNY *throws her wallet at him.*)

Help yourself – you're having a lucky day, I just went to the bank...

ZEKE. I'm sorry!

I'm sorry, Jenny.

(pause)

Why didn't you call me on it?

JENNY. Because I thought we made each other feel better.

Because I wanted you to give it back before I left, to run after me when I was going down the block; I didn't want to come home to my empty apartment thinking about what you did again and again like it was bouncing off the walls!

(pause)

ZEKE. I'm sorry.

I'm joining a program.

JENNY. For what?

ZEKE. For a little peace.

JENNY. I wish you luck.

(pause)

ZEKE. I was hoping you'd come by later, and we'd order in some Chinese food.

JENNY. *(disbelief)* What?

Why?

ZEKE. Fatten you up a bit, you're awfully skinny.

JENNY. Shouldn't I stay far away from you?

ZEKE. I get the feeling you don't always make the best decisions.

(pause)

JENNY. Why are you suddenly acting all healthy and normal?

ZEKE. It's a goal of mine.

JENNY. I've had the same goal for years.

ZEKE. How's that going?

JENNY. Excellent. Can't you see how well adjusted I am?

(ZEKE laughs.)

What's changed you?

ZEKE. *(after a moment)* I'm scared.

Scared that a park bench will become my home.

(pause)

I understand if you don't want to see me.

(no response)

Think about it. I'll leave the money here.

(ZEKE puts the money on a table.)

That path I'm on, my yellow brick road, you were right – I don't know how it ends.

(They hold each other's stare.)

I hope I haven't blown it with you, Jenny.

JENNY. You can't just crush me like that and think you can come over and get me back.

ZEKE. *(after a moment)* I'll woo you.

JENNY. You'll woo me?

ZEKE. I've wanted to say it, but, you know...

JENNY. Talking about feelings isn't your forte.

ZEKE. When I wrote that note...

When I wrote you that note, I kept wondering what would have happened if your father didn't exist, if we were just two people stumbling across each other in this crowded and lonely city – I kept thinking how good things might have turned out.

JENNY. *(after a moment – quiet)* That's a quality woo.

ZEKE. It's meant most sincerely.

(pause)

JENNY. Do you want to stay? We can rent a movie.

ZEKE. I have to clean up.

And I need to go for a run, start getting in shape. Not sure how far I'll get, but, you know, it's only day one.

I figure by the time I'm done running and showering, you'll arrive. Or I can come back...

JENNY. I'll come to your place. Nine o'clock?

ZEKE. Yeah, that sounds good.

(They hold each other's stare.)

I'm gonna get through this.

JENNY. I hope you do.

(joking)

I figure if a messed up guy like you can recover, who knows what glories may be in store for me.

(ZEKE laughs.)

What you said before, about the park bench being your home, you can't ever let that happen. If things ever got that bad, I'd help you, Zeke. I'd help you no matter what happens between us.

ZEKE. I appreciate that.

I'll see you later.

(After a moment, ZEKE walks over to JENNY and kisses her. It is almost awkward.)

All right then.

(ZEKE leaves.)

(After a moment, JENNY follows ZEKE to the door. She stops, feeling good.)

(She then picks the money up and puts it in her wallet. She holds it against her – life has such promise. She puts the wallet in her bag and sits – day-dreaming.)

(The lights slowly come down, except for a "Special Light" which holds on JENNY for a few beats.)

(lights down)

(end scene)

Scene V

(The apartment has been cleaned and is spotless. ZEKE *has showered and looks like a new man. He has set up a large fish tank and is placing an ornament in it when* MARTIN *enters wearing gloves, locking the door behind him.)*

MARTIN. You should keep your door locked.

(ZEKE stops what he is doing and stares at MARTIN.*)*

Dangerous city.

ZEKE. Don't remember inviting you for dinner.

MARTIN. Don't remember inviting you for a late night snack.

ZEKE. Get out…

MARTIN. Not yet…

ZEKE. Things are over between…

MARTIN. They will be.

*(*MARTIN *pulls out a gun.)*

ZEKE. You gonna try and make me hop up and down?

MARTIN. No.

(pause)

(ZEKE adds a boat to his tank.)

ZEKE. Sunken pirate ship – looks good, right?

(no response)

You like fish?

MARTIN. To eat.

ZEKE. They keep me calm – beautiful creatures. Maybe all you need is a fish tank.

(no response)

You enter a man's home with a gun drawn, and it's a sure sign you need to relax…

MARTIN. *(exploding)* What the fuck did you think I would do!

(pause)

ZEKE. Like you said, both our lives end with that trigger.

MARTIN. Like you said, I have to look in the mirror.

ZEKE. You'll be able to do that with a dead man on your…

MARTIN. What choice did you leave?

ZEKE. You walk away.

MARTIN. And let you strike again?

Let you knock on my daughter's door?

(pause)

ZEKE. You don't want to enter my world. You don't want to live here.

MARTIN. I won't be living here; I'll only be visiting.

ZEKE. Wish it were that simple. Wish you could just shower and wash all that dirt and sweat and crap out of you. No one gets off that easy.

MARTIN. You're an ex-con with a violent past – that creates a lot of enemies, a lot of possible suspects…

ZEKE. People know about our history.

MARTIN. I let go of Ralph, my security personnel today. He wanted to kill you himself…

ZEKE. Why didn't you let him?

MARTIN. I handle my own crap.

And maybe he's not as good as he says, leaves a few breadcrumbs, and they get to him. Maybe he strikes a deal for a reduced sentence.

So, yes, he wanted to take care of you, but I said, no, it's over, that I should've never gotten you fired…

ZEKE. You shouldn't have.

MARTIN. Of course I should – you're a psycho.

ZEKE. Who's holding the gun?

MARTIN. *(after a moment)* I told him if he does anything, I'll testify against him – I just might have to do that anyway, tell the police about his tenacity.

ZEKE. You're a helluvan employer.

MARTIN. He'll be fine. He hasn't done anything.

But, most importantly, he'll testify to everything I've said.

(pause)

ZEKE. Walk away, Martin, leave it alone…

MARTIN. When you were pummeling me, holding that gun at my head, I'm thinking at least it's me…

ZEKE. Get the hell out…

MARTIN. At least I'm the one you're attacking, devastating…

ZEKE. *(approaching)* Don't fucking push me!

MARTIN. I have the gun now!

> (**MARTIN** *points the gun at* **ZEKE**, *stopping him in his tracks.*)

Take one more step, one more fucking step!

ZEKE. *(after a moment)* No, no it's not gonna be that easy. You're gonna have to look me in the eye, look me in the eye when you squeeze that trigger.

MARTIN. *(quiet)* You've left me no choice. You'll get another job rejection and come hunting me and mine.

ZEKE. Go to the police; if that's your fear…

MARTIN. I know I can protect myself, make myself impenetrable, and it does me no good, not one bit of good. I keep hearing Ralph's voice telling me that my daughter is sitting there, sitting there with a bullseye on her.

(after a moment)

I didn't want it to come to this.

ZEKE. I don't either.

(pause)

What time is it?

MARTIN. What does that matter?

ZEKE. Want to know the hour of my death.

MARTIN. Ten after nine.

ZEKE. How do you think you'll feel killing me?

(no response)

ZEKE. How do you…

MARTIN. Don't imagine I'll be feeling very good.

ZEKE. Probably better than me.

What are you going to do after you leave?

MARTIN. Time to get this over with.

(MARTIN *raises the gun and points it at* ZEKE.)

ZEKE. Can I feed the fish first? Could be a while before my body's found.

MARTIN. *(after a moment)* Go ahead.

(MARTIN *lowers the gun.*)

ZEKE. Do me a favor, after you kill me, don't eat my fish.

(ZEKE *feeds the fish.*)

All this because of dust.

MARTIN. Because of dust.

(MARTIN *again raises the gun. They hold each other's stare.*)

(A moment)

ZEKE. If you do this, there's no going back, starting over, there's no twelve step program for murderers.

(no response)

I'd never hurt your daughter...

MARTIN. I didn't grow up on Fifth Avenue...

ZEKE. I want a chance at fixing my life...

MARTIN. I know when danger's in the room!

ZEKE. A chance at living my life...

MARTIN. No, no...

ZEKE. Give me that chance, Martin...

MARTIN. Shut-up...

ZEKE. I'm a different man now...

MARTIN. Shut the fuck up!

(mumbling) I need to think...

(MARTIN *steps away, lowering the gun.*)

ZEKE. For the first time in a long time, I'm excited about what lays ahead.

(no response)

ZEKE. *(cont.)* All this shit that's happened between us, that I've been going through, I'm turning something bad into something positive...

MARTIN. Prove it.

ZEKE. I'm a better man...

MARTIN. It's not possible to prove!

It's not possible because I've tried. I tell myself, I can live with the beat down, that nothing really bad happened. But your voice is there haunting me, telling me someone is going to die, and Ralph's voice telling me it'll be my daughter, and that there's no choice, no fucking choice!

(quiet) It's not possible to prove.

(After a moment, ZEKE picks up a pamphlet, of which there are a few, lying on his table.)

ZEKE. *(reading)* "We have found hope. We can learn to..."

MARTIN. What the hell is that?

ZEKE. A pamphlet from N.A.

MARTIN. N.A.?

ZEKE. Narcotics Anonymous.

MARTIN. You belong?

ZEKE. I go to my first meeting tomorrow, six p.m.

MARTIN. A different man?

ZEKE. A better man.

(reading) "We can learn to function in the world in which we live. We can find meaning and purpose in life and be rescued from insanity, depravity, and death."

(a beat)

(The apartment buzzer rings.)

(No one moves.)

(It rings again.)

MARTIN. Don't move. Let them leave.

ZEKE. She's here.

MARTIN. Who?

ZEKE. You're daughter.

MARTIN. What? My…

ZEKE. Daughter

We have a date.

(no response)

Chinese food and a movie.

(After a moment, the buzzer rings again.)

MARTIN. *(quiet)* I can't let you touch her.

ZEKE. Let her in, let her talk to you.

MARTIN. Talk to me?

(ZEKE starts walking towards the buzzer, holding MARTIN's stare the entire time.)

ZEKE. This is our last chance, Martin, our last chance to say this is who I was yesterday…

MARTIN. You can't get close to her…

ZEKE. This is who I was yesterday, but it's not who I'm gonna be.

MARTIN. You placed a gun against my head…

ZEKE. I'm just gonna let her in…

MARTIN. It could have been her, it could have been her head…

(ZEKE is at the buzzer and is about to respond, when MARTIN shoots him. ZEKE goes down.)

(A moment. MARTIN is frozen.)

(The buzzer rings again, as the lights blackout, except for a special on ZEKE's dead body.)

(Darkness, as the sound of the buzzer increases, echoing throughout the theatre.)

(silence)

(end scene)

End of Play

PROPS

WHAT	CHARA.	NOTES
Act I, scene 1		*Essex House Gym*
Newspaper	Zeke	*Daily News*
Treadmill	Martin	-light, easy to move
Sports bottle	Martin	-high-end
Phone	Zeke	-hotel-style
Towel	Martin	-sweat towel
Act I, scene 2		*Zeke's Apartment*
Garbage Can		
Small Plastic Hose	Bobby	In garbage pail -tubing like used in a fish tank -mistaken for drug paraphernalia
Linda Tynes' Information	Bobby	(written on business card stock)
Act I, scene 3		*Zeke's Apartment*
K-Mart shopping bag	Zeke	-holds Dust Buster
Radio/ CD player combo	Zeke	-possibly clock radio/CD player
(2) Beers	Zeke	-opened and consumed each performance -Budweiser
Journal (or) Datebook	Jenny	In purse -pages able to be written on and torn out
Pen	Jenny	In purse
Dust Buster	Zeke	In shopping bag -in box?
Act I, scene 4		*Martin's Apartment*
Vase of Flowers	Dressing	

Silver Coffee service:
    Tray
    Coffee Carafe
    (2) Coffee Mugs
	Ralph
	Martin
		-hotel style

Ice Bucket	Dressing	-not used
Decanter of Whiskey		-1/2 filled w/ apple juice
Decanter of Vodka		-3/4 filled w/ water (not used)
(2) Drinking glasses		-number unknown; for alcohol
Dust Buster	Jenny	-not in box; from I-3
Shoulder bag	Jenny	-fits Dust Buster
Act I, scene 5		*Zeke's Apartment*
Notepad w/ writing on page	Zeke	-beginning of letter to Jenny -on table; steno-size notepad
Pen	Zeke	-on table
Several crumpled pieces of paper		-on table
Small fish bowl w/ (2) Fish	Bobby	-catfish & angel fish
Container of fish food	Bobby	-has fish food; fish get fed
Act I, scene 6		*Street / V.O. Section*
Automatic Gun #1	Man	-fake; non-firing; *no clip*
Act I, scene 7		*Martin's Apartment*
Bottle of Viagra	Zeke	-contains few pills; bottle not opened
Automatic Gun #1	Zeke	-from I-6

PROPS

WHAT	CHARA.	NOTES
Act II, scene 1		**Digs' Apartment into Park**
(2) Beers	Digs	-opened and consumed each performanc -Corona (apple juice & water)
Automatic Gun #2	Zeke	-non-firing; gun *w/ clip*
Gold Cigarette Case w/ Joints	Digs	-contains (8) joints -need rolling papers & herbal tobacco -1 joint smoked per performance
Torch Lighter	Digs	-practical -Digs & Zeke should have back-up light
Eight Ball of Meth	Digs	-smoked on stage
Pipe (for smoking Meth)	Digs	-used to smoke crack; packed w/ tobacco
Act II, scene 2		**Zeke's Apartment**
(2) $20 bills	Zeke	-in Jenny's wallet
Gucci Wallet	Zeke	-in Jenny's purse
Purse		
Partial Baggie of Meth	Zeke	-small amount of crystal; not used
Act II, scene 3		**Bobby's Patio / Switch Focus Scene**
Hose on Storage holder	Dressing	
(2) Baseball mitts	Bobby	-in outdoor chest -fits Zeke & Bobby
Baseball	Bobby	-in outdoor chest
Plastic Pipe	Zeke	-can be dropped without breaking
Vial of Meth w/ 1 hit left	Zeke	-Meth smoked in pipe
Torch Lighter	Zeke	
Revolver in Wooden Gun Box	Martin	In drawer of table (Martin's apt) -practical; fires blanks
Act II, scene 4		**Jenny's Apartment**
(2) $20 Bills	Zeke	-from II-2
Gucci Wallet	Jenny	-in purse
Purse	Jenny	
Act II, scene 5		**Zeke's Apartment**
Large fish tank w/ Fish *See note at end*	Zeke	-10 gallon tank w/ rocks, plants, filter, heater & several fish -some of the fish should match bowl
Sunken pirate ship (for fish tank)	Zeke	-placed in tank each performance by acto
(3) N.A. pamphlets	Zeke	-Narcotics Anonymous
Fake Blood in Syringe	Crew	-squirted through crack in walls onto act back

**Fish for bowl in I-5 are kept in a storage 10 gallon tank. Fish for II-5 live in stage tan

COSTUME PROPS

Bobby's Wallet
Purse
Briefcase (or) Attaché
Backpack
Handkerchief
Jenny's Wallet
Motorcycle helmet
Sexy lingerie

FURNITURE

Gym
Table (*used in all scenes)
Green Chair
Treadmill
Zeke's Apt
Futon
Side Table
Sink
Wooden Chair
Table
Brown Refrigerator
Martin's Apt
(2) Black Leather Armchairs
Mini-bar
Side Table
Jenny's Apt
Dressing table w/ matching Stool
Digs' Apt
Table
(2) Metal Rattan Chairs
Black Refrigerator
Bobby's Patio
Outdoor ches

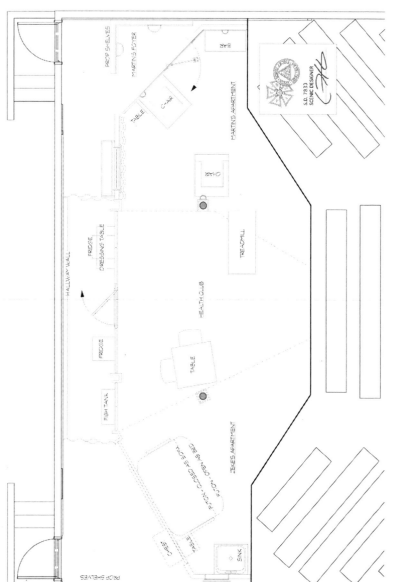

Dust Set Design: 1-1
Copyright © 2008 by Caleb Wertenbaker

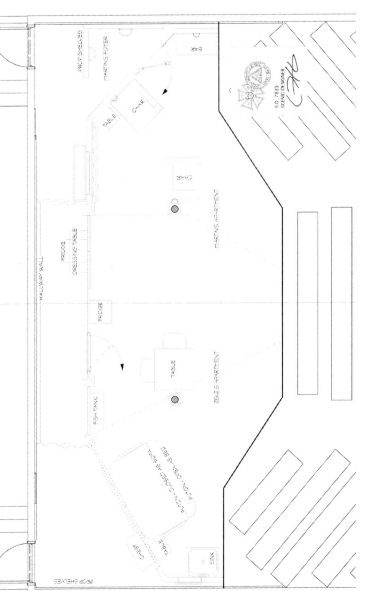

Dust Set Design: 1-II, 1-III and 1-IV
Copyright © 2008 by Caleb Wertenbaker

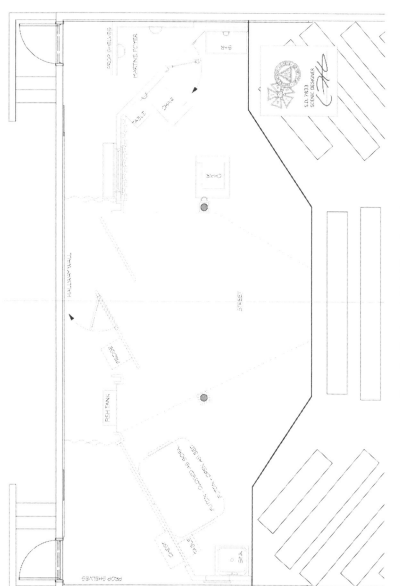

Dust Set Design: 1-V, 1-VI and 1-VII

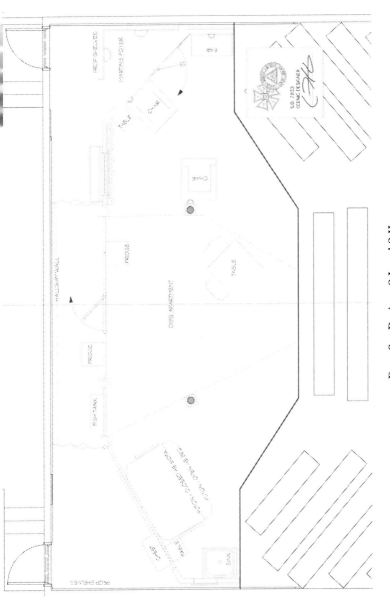

Dust Set Design: 2-I and 2-II
Copyright © 2008 by Caleb Wertenbaker

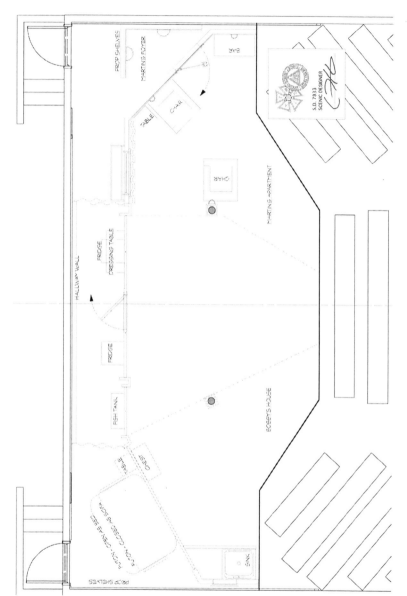

Dust Set Design: 2-III
Copyright © 2008 by Caleb Wertenbaker

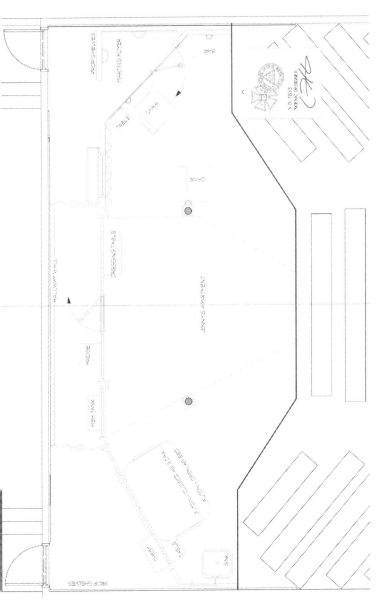

Dust Set Design: 2-IV and 2-V
Copyright © 2008 by Caleb Wertenbaker

OTHER TITLES AVAILABLE FROM SAMUEL FRENCH

EURYDICE
Sarah Ruhl

Dramatic Comedy / 5m, 2f / Unit Set

In *Eurydice*, Sarah Ruhl re-imagines the classic myth of Orpheus through the eyes of its heroine. Dying too young on her wedding day, Eurydice must journey to the underworld, where she reunites with her father and struggles to remember her lost love. With contemporary characters, ingenious plot twists, and breathtaking visual effects, the play is a fresh look at a timeless love story.

"RHAPSODICALLY BEAUTIFUL...a weird and wonderful new play - an inexpressibly moving theatrical fable about love, loss and the pleasures and pains of memory."
- *The New York Times*

"EXHILARATING!! A luminous retelling of the Orpheus myth, lush and limpid as a dream where both author and audience swim in the magical, sometimes menacing, and always thrilling flow of the unconscious."
- *The New Yorker*

"Exquisitely staged by Les Waters and an inventive design team... Ruhl's wild flights of imagination, some deeply affecting passages and beautiful imagery provide transporting pleasures. They conspire to create original, at times breathtaking, stage pictures."
- *Variety*

"Touching, inventive, invigoratingly compact and luminously liquid in its rhythms and design, *Eurydice* reframes the ancient myth of ill-fated love to focus not on the bereaved musician but on his dead bride – and on her struggle with love beyond the grave as both wife and daughter."
- *The San Francisco Chronicle*

SAMUELFRENCH.COM

OTHER TITLES AVAILABLE FROM SAMUEL FRENCH

EVIL DEAD: THE MUSICAL
Book & Lyrics By George Reinblatt
Music By Frank Cipolla/Christopher Bond/Melissa Morris/
George Reinblatt

Musical Comedy / 6m, 4f / Unit set
Based on Sam Raimi's 80s cult classic films, *Evil Dead* tells the
tale of five college kids who travel to a cabin in the woods
and accidentally unleash an evil force. And although it may
sound like a horror, it's not! The songs are hilariously campy
and the show is bursting with more farce than a Monty Py-
thon skit. *Evil Dead: The Musical* unearths the old familiar
story: boy and friends take a weekend getaway at abandoned
cabin, boy expects to get lucky, boy unleashes ancient evil
spirit, friends turn into Candarian Demons, boy fights un-
til dawn to survive. As musical mayhem descends upon this
sleepover in the woods, "camp" takes on a whole new meaning with uproarious numbers like "All the Men in my Life
Keep Getting Killed by Candarian Demons," "Look Who's
Evil Now" and "Do the Necronomicon."

**Outer Critics Circle nomination for
Outstanding New Off-Broadway Musical**

"The next Rocky Horror Show!"
- *The New York Times*

"A ridiculous amount of fun."
- *Variety*

"Wickedly campy good time."
- *The Associated Press*

LaVergne, TN USA
19 August 2009
155331LV00001B/9/P

9 780573 696527